A Tradition *of* Taste

Healthy, Exotic, and Simple to Prepare Cuisine
from the Land of the Bible

BOOKMARK PUBLISHING

DALLAS, TEXAS

A Tradition of Taste
Jacqueline Overpeck, General Editor
© 2007 Bookmark Publishing

Published by Bookmark Publishing
Dallas, Texas

All oven tempoeratures are based on the Fahrenheit scale.

www.BennyHinn.org

ISBN 1-59024-300-5

Printed in the United States of America

First Edition 2007

10 9 8 7 6 5 4 3 2 1

Contents

Foreword

Do you not know that your body is the temple of the
Holy Spirit who is in you, whom you have from God?
1 CORINTHIANS 6:19

A *Tradition of Taste* is a collection of exotic recipes from the land of the Bible! Since my childhood in Jaffa, the food of that region has been an important and memorable part of my life. Throughout the land of the Bible and the entire Middle East, food has always been central to hospitality.

The Bible is filled with examples of friendly meals and family feasts, all with the robust and healthy foods prepared on hometown hearths, and those traditions continue to this day. With *A Tradition of Taste*, you can now enjoy many of the same favorite recipes from the land of my childhood! All recipes marked with a special symbol are family recipes contributed by my own mother, Clemence Hinn.

Whether you are an experienced cook or just a beginner, these exotic dishes will enable you and your family to experience the robust flavors of the Middle East, Greece, the Mediterranean, Lebanon, Egypt, and Israel—right in your own kitchen.

Throughout *A Tradition of Taste* you'll find tantalizing dishes that feature specially selected ingredients used for centuries in the Holy Land, many of which are mentioned in the Bible. Recipes such as tabbouleh, smoked salmon salad, cream of Jerusalem artichoke soup, and olive-stuffed grape leaves will soon be among your favorites, as they are mine.

You'll enjoy preparing Laban Immu, Middle Eastern platters with falafel, and baklava. You can discover the phenomenal traditional dishes of some of the Bible's richest life-giving food resources right from the recipes you now hold in your hands.

Many of these recipes, such as hamantashen, triangular-shaped Jewish pastries, are ideal for making with children. No matter whether you use these recipes to create new family traditions or to delight friends at your next church fellowship dinner, I know you'll find each wonderful recipe satisfying.

I pray that this special collection of exciting recipes, celebrating the historic cuisine of the Middle East—the land of the Bible—will help you do just that. Enjoy!

—BENNY HINN

I

APPETIZERS

Tabbouleh

½ cup fine-grain cracked wheat (bulgur)

½ cup green onions, finely chopped (4 onions)

3 cups parsley, finely chopped (2 bunches)

2 cups tomatoes, finely chopped (not too ripe)

1 cup cucumbers, finely chopped baby (optional)

½ cup fresh mint leaves, finely chopped

½ cup fresh lemon juice, or to taste

¾ cup olive oil

1 teaspoon salt, or to taste

Head of romaine lettuce

Wash parsley well, drain, and shake out excess moisture. Rinse the cracked wheat in a bowl, then cover with water by ½-inch and let soak for 5 minutes. Drain well, squeezing out excess water. Set aside while preparing other ingredients. Remove stems from parsley and discard. Chop parsley very fine (2 bunches should equal about 3 cups). Add to cracked wheat. Chop green onions fine and add to mixture. Add the remaining ingredients. Toss well. Serve on romaine lettuce, torn into bite-sized pieces.

Hummus (Chickpea Tahini Dip)

1 can (15-ounce) chickpeas (garbanzos)

3 tablespoons tahini (sesame paste)

2–3 cloves garlic, pressed or crushed (fresh, no substitutes!)

1–2 lemons, juiced and strained

Salt, to taste

Olive oil

Paprika

Olive

Pine nuts (optional)

Drain the canned chickpeas, reserving some of the liquid. You may reserve a few whole chickpeas for garnish. Rinse away the taste of the can with fresh water. Combine chickpeas, garlic, and tahini in a food processor and blend; add lemon juice gradually. The mixture should become smooth and spreadable but thick. Add some of the reserved liquid as required. Salt sparingly if using canned, pre-salted chickpeas. Dish into a shallow bowl. Sprinkle with paprika; garnish with an olive or a few reserved whole chickpeas; drizzle with best-quality olive oil. Serve at room temperature with pita bread cut into triangles. Optional garnish: Pine nuts sautéed in butter until barely brown.

Note: To substitute dried chickpeas for canned chickpeas, soak a cup of dried chickpeas overnight, drain, then cover generously with water and simmer until tender. Depending on the age of the legume, this could take 2 hours. Reserve some of the cooking water; let cool.

BULGUR AND LENTIL GRUEL WITH PINE NUTS

1 package (8.8-ounce) brown lentils, washed and well drained

1 package (8.8-ounce) coarse bulgur, washed and well drained

1 small onion, chopped

2½ ounces olive oil

2 large onions, sliced into thin rings

¼ cup pine nuts, toasted

3 cloves garlic, minced

1 quart water

Salt and pepper, to taste

In a large saucepan, cover lentils with water and boil 45 minutes or until almost cooked. Drain and reserve the cooking liquid. In a heavy-bottomed pot, heat 1 tablespoon of the olive oil. Add the small chopped onion and sauté until golden brown. Add washed bulgur, lentils, salt, and 1 pint of water. Simmer 20 to 25 minutes or until all liquid has evaporated. Remove from heat; let stand 10 minutes. Heat remaining oil in a large skillet. Add sliced onion rings, toasted pine nuts, and minced garlic. Sauté until golden brown. Place bulgur and lentil gruel on serving dish; top with sautéed onion, pine nuts, and garlic mixture.

FIGS AND HONEY WITH TOASTED ALMONDS OVER BRIE

½ cup honey

6 fresh figs, stemmed and quartered

½ cup toasted almonds

½ teaspoon vanilla extract

1 (14-ounce) round Brie cheese

Preheat oven to 325 degrees. Heat honey in a small saucepan over low heat until warm and melted. Add figs and cook until softened, about 10 minutes. Stir in almonds and vanilla. Place Brie in baking dish. Cover with fig and honey mixture. Bake in preheated oven for 10 to 15 minutes, or until softened but not melted. Serve warm with your favorite crackers.

Mediterranean Spinach Pita Pizza

2 (8-inch) pita bread rounds

1 teaspoon olive oil

1 cup canned cannelloni beans, rinsed and drained

2 teaspoons lemon juice

2 teaspoons red wine vinegar or cider vinegar

Black pepper

2 medium cloves garlic, minced

¼ cup thinly sliced radicchio or escarole lettuce

¼ cup torn fresh spinach

½ cup chopped seeded tomato

¼ cup finely chopped red onion

¼ cup (1-ounce) crumbled feta cheese

2 tablespoons thinly sliced pitted black olives

Preheat oven to 450 degrees. Place pita on baking sheet; brush with olive oil. Bake 4 to 6 minutes. Mash cannelloni beans with fork. Stir in lemon juice, vinegar, minced garlic, and dash of black pepper. Spread bean mixture on pita. Top with radicchio or lettuce, spinach, tomato, onion, feta cheese, and olives. Bake 5 minutes or until topping is heated through. Cheese will be slightly melted and crust crisp. Cut into pizza-shaped wedges to serve.

Roasted Spinach, Cheese, and Garlic Rolls

3 cups fresh spinach leaves, shredded

¾ cup (3 ounces) crumbled feta cheese

½ cup (2 ounces) shredded Monterey Jack cheese

4–5 fresh garlic cloves, minced

1 teaspoon dried oregano

1 teaspoon dried dill weed

¼ teaspoon black pepper

7 (7-inch) flour tortillas

Preheat oven to 375 degrees. Place spinach, cheese, and garlic in medium bowl. Add oregano, dill weed, and black pepper to the mixture. Combine all ingredients, mix well. Spread spinach mixture evenly onto tortillas and roll up. Cut roll into 1-inch slices. Place slices, cut sides up onto nonstick baking sheet. Bake 10 to 14 minutes until golden. Serve warm or at room temperature.

SMOKED SALMON AND EGG SALAD

12 eggs, boiled, peeled, chopped

2 stalks celery, chopped

½ cup frozen peas, thawed

1 red onion, chopped

5 ounces diced smoked salmon

1 cup mayonnaise

1 teaspoon Dijon mustard

3 tablespoons chopped fresh dill

⅛ teaspoon ground red pepper

Salt and black pepper, to taste

Toast rounds or other low-fat crackers

In a medium bowl, combine eggs, celery, peas, onion, smoked salmon, mayonnaise, and mustard. Season with dill, red pepper, salt, and black pepper. Refrigerate for several hours to allow flavors to combine. Spoon mixture onto toast rounds or low-fat crackers to serve.

Greek Fig, Feta, and Olive Spread

5 fresh figs

1 (6-ounce) package feta cheese, crumbled

2½ tablespoons olive oil

1 teaspoon lemon juice

½ teaspoon minced garlic

2 ounces sun-dried tomatoes, softened

½ teaspoon dried oregano

½ teaspoon dried rosemary

1 tablespoon chopped black olives, drained

Place figs, feta cheese, olive oil, lemon juice, garlic, sun-dried tomatoes, oregano, and rosemary in a food processor. Blend until smooth and scrape into in a bowl. Stir in the olives. Refrigerate until serving.

Matboucha

2 tablespoons olive oil

5 cloves garlic, peeled and pressed

2 green peppers, seeded and diced

7 ripe tomatoes

½ to 1 teaspoon paprika

½ to 1 teaspoon black pepper

Salt, to taste

Pita bread or crackers

Heat olive oil in a skillet over medium heat. Add garlic and peppers. Cook until tender, stir frequently. Add tomatoes, paprika, black pepper, and salt. Cook uncovered for 30 minutes, or until most of liquid evaporates. Serve with pita bread or your favorite crackers.

2

SOUPS

Lentil Soup

1½ cup lentils (regular, not red)

7 cups water

1 medium yellow onion, chopped

5 cloves garlic, halved

1 tablespoon olive oil

1 teaspoon salt

Freshly ground black pepper, to taste

1 lemon

Go through and remove any stones from lentils. Rinse well. In a large soup pot, place all ingredients except lemon juice, salt, and pepper. Bring to a boil, then reduce heat and simmer. When the lentils have cooked for about 45 minutes, add salt and pepper to taste. Simmer for another 20 minutes or so until tender. The soup will thicken. Just before serving, add about half the lemon juice, then taste to see whether you want to add the rest. Add more salt and/or pepper to taste.

CREAM OF JERUSALEM ARTICHOKE SOUP

¼ cup (½ stick) unsalted butter

2 onions, minced

1 pound Jerusalem artichokes, roughly chopped

2 potatoes, peeled and cubed

3 dried portobello mushrooms, softened in water

1 tablespoon rice vinegar

1 tablespoon flour

3 cups chicken broth

¾ cup heavy whipping cream

½ teaspoon ground black pepper

½ teaspoon salt

¼ cup chopped fresh parsley

Melt butter in a large saucepan over medium heat. Add onions, artichokes, potatoes, and mushrooms. Cook, covered, over low heat for 10 minutes. Uncover and cook for an additional 8 minutes. Stir in rice vinegar and flour and cook for 1 minute. Gradually stir in about 2 cups of the broth. Stir continuously, until the soup boils and thickens. Simmer another 5 minutes. Transfer to a food processor and puree until smooth, adding more broth as needed. Return the soup to the pan and add cream, ground black pepper, and salt. Reheat. Ladle into soup bowls and garnish with the chopped parsley.

LAMB AND BEAN VEGETABLE STEW

2 tablespoons olive oil

1 pound lamb stew meat, cubed

2 cups beef broth

1 cup cider vinegar

2 cloves garlic, minced

1 tablespoon chopped fresh thyme

¼ teaspoon salt

¼ teaspoon black pepper

1 bay leaf

¼ pound great Northern or white beans

2 cups butternut squash, peeled, seeded, and sliced

1 cup parsnips, peeled, sliced

1 cup sweet potatoes, peeled, chopped

1 cup celery, sliced

1 medium onion, thinly sliced

½ cup sour cream

3 tablespoons flour

Heat olive oil in a large saucepan. Add lamb and brown meat on all sides. Drain fat, and stir in the beef broth and cider vinegar. Season with garlic, thyme, salt, pepper, and bay leaf. Bring mixture to a boil. Reduce heat, cover, and simmer 20 minutes. Transfer seasoned meat to a pot. Mix in the beans, squash, parsnips, sweet potatoes, celery, and onion. Bring to a boil, then reduce heat and simmer 30 minutes, or until tender. In a small bowl, blend sour cream and flour. Stir into the hot stew mixture. Remove the bay leaf. Continue cooking, stirring occasionally until stew is thickened.

Mediterranean Fisherman Stew

4 cloves garlic, minced

2 onions, chopped

1 tablespoon olive oil

1 (28-ounce) can crushed tomatoes

6 cups water

½ cup chopped fresh parsley

½ cup chopped fresh cilantro

2 tablespoons Worcestershire sauce

1 teaspoon ground cinnamon

1 teaspoon paprika

1½ pounds cod fillets, cubed

3 ounces dry pasta

½ cup kalamata olives, pitted and sliced

¼ cup almonds, chopped

¼ teaspoon ground black pepper

¼ teaspoon salt

In a large pot over medium heat, sauté garlic and onions in olive oil for 5 minutes, stirring constantly. Pour in tomatoes with their liquid; add water, parsley, and cilantro. Bring to a boil, then reduce heat to low. Simmer 15 minutes. Stir in the Worcestershire sauce, cinnamon, paprika, and fish. Simmer over medium heat for 10 minutes. Add pasta, olives, and almonds. Simmer an additional 8 minutes, or until pasta is tender. Stir in salt and pepper.

GARLIC AND SPINACH SOUP

2 tablespoons olive oil

4 cloves garlic, peeled and crushed

1 medium onion, coarsely chopped

4 leeks, chopped

2 teaspoons ground cumin

2 teaspoons ground coriander

1⅓ quarts vegetable stock

3 medium potatoes, peeled and chopped

1 cup heavy cream

2 tablespoons tahini

2 tablespoons cornmeal

½ pound spinach, rinsed and chopped

Ground cayenne pepper, to taste

Salt, to taste

Heat olive oil in a large pot over medium heat. Add garlic, onion, and leeks. Cook until tender. Season with cumin and coriander. Pour vegetable stock and potatoes into the pot and bring to a boil. Reduce heat and simmer about 10 minutes. In a small bowl, blend the heavy cream, tahini, and cornmeal. Mix into the soup. Stir spinach into the soup. Season with cayenne pepper and salt. Cook until spinach is heated through.

Egyptian Fava Bean Soup

1 cup onions, chopped

2 garlic cloves, minced

1½ teaspoons ground cumin seeds

1½ teaspoons sweet Hungarian paprika

¼ teaspoon cayenne

1 bay leaf

¼ cup cilantro, finely chopped

1 large carrot, chopped

1½ cups fresh tomatoes, chopped

4 cups vegetable stock

2 (15-ounce) cans fava beans, rinsed and drained

¼ cup chopped fresh parsley

3 tablespoons fresh lemon juice

Salt and freshly ground black pepper to taste

In a large soup pot, sauté onions and garlic until the onions are tender. Add cumin, paprika, cayenne, bay leaf, cilantro, and carrots. Cook on medium heat for several minutes. Stir in tomatoes and vegetable stock. Simmer 15 minutes over medium heat until the carrots are soft. Add the fava beans, parsley, and lemon juice. Add salt and pepper to taste.

Spinach and Chickpea Soup

4 cups water

2 cups uncooked brown rice

1 tablespoon olive oil

1 medium onion, finely chopped

2 garlic cloves, minced

8 ounces fresh shiitake mushrooms, thinly sliced

6 cups vegetable broth

¼ teaspoon dried rosemary, finely chopped

¼ teaspoon cilantro, finely chopped

1 (15-ounce) can chickpeas, drained and rinsed

3 carrots, peeled and finely chopped

2 (5-ounce) bags baby spinach leaves

Coarse salt and freshly ground pepper

½ cup freshly grated Parmesan cheese

In a large saucepan, bring water to a boil. Stir in rice and return to a boil; then reduce to simmer. Cook, covered, for 30 minutes. Meanwhile, in another large saucepan, heat oil over medium heat. Add onion; cook until tender. Add garlic and mushrooms, cooking until mushrooms are tender. Add broth, rosemary, and cilantro; bring to a boil. Cover and remove from heat. Check rice; if it isn't done, cook an additional 10 minutes. Add 2 cups of the cooked rice, the chickpeas, and carrots and stir into broth; return to a boil. Reduce to simmer, cover, and cook for 5 more minutes to allow flavors to blend. Stir in spinach. Cook, uncovered, just until spinach is wilted, about 1 minute. Season with salt and pepper. Garnish with Parmesan cheese. Serve hot.

Mediterranean Pasta E Fagioli Soup

1 tablespoons olive oil

1 medium onion, diced

2 stalks celery, tops removed, sliced

2 large carrots, peeled and sliced

2 cloves garlic, minced

4 cups low-fat chicken broth

1 (15-ounce) can white beans, undrained

1 (15-ounce) can red kidney beans, undrained

1 (14-ounce) can diced Italian tomatoes

1 bay leaf

1 teaspoon dried basil

½ teaspoon oregano

1 cup small shell pasta

1 medium eggplant, peeled and diced

¼ cup parsley, chopped

Salt and freshly ground pepper to taste

1 cup Parmesan cheese, freshly grated

Heat olive oil in a soup pot. Add onions, celery, and carrots. Sauté on low heat for 5 minutes. Add garlic; continue cooking for 2 minutes. Add broth, white beans, kidney beans, tomatoes, bay leaf, basil, and oregano. Simmer for 10 minutes. Add pasta, eggplant, and parsley. Cook until pasta is done. Add more broth if needed. Add salt and pepper to taste. Ladle into bowls. Garnish with Parmesan cheese.

SPICY TOMATO AND EGGPLANT SOUP

6 tablespoons olive oil

1 medium onion, finely chopped

1 medium eggplant, peeled and cubed

1½ sprigs fresh oregano

1 (14-ounce) can diced tomatoes, in juice

3 cloves garlic, minced

1 small fresh or dried red chili pepper, seeds removed for less heat

1 carrot, peeled and thinly sliced

1½ cups plain soy milk

1 tablespoon fresh lemon juice

Coarse salt and ground pepper to taste

Heat 3 tablespoons olive oil; add onions, eggplant, and oregano, and sauté five minutes. Heat broiler. Strain tomatoes, reserving the juice. Spread tomatoes on a rimmed baking sheet; drizzle with 3 tablespoons olive oil. Broil tomatoes 6 to 9 minutes. Combine browned tomatoes, garlic, chili pepper, carrot, soy milk, reserved tomato juice, and lemon juice in a food processor. Blend until smooth. Transfer ingredients to a saucepan, then add sautéed onions and eggplant mixture. Bring soup to a boil over medium heat. Reduce to a simmer. Season with salt and pepper.

Vegetarian Jewish Cabbage and Potato Soup

6 tablespoons olive oil

1 medium cabbage, shredded

2 cups potatoes, diced

2 medium onions, chopped

2 tablespoons flour

2 teaspoons salt

½ teaspoon pepper

6 cups water

3 cups tomato juice

2 tablespoons sugar

1 teaspoon caraway seeds

1 carton sour cream

Heat olive oil in soup pot. Add cabbage, potatoes, and onions. Cook for about 20 minutes, or until soft. Add flour, salt, pepper, water, tomato juice, sugar, and caraway seeds. Cook uncovered on low heat for 55 to 60 minutes. Ladle into serving bowels, and garnish with a dollop of sour cream.

3

SALADS

Cucumber and Yogurt Salad

1 medium or 2–3 small cucumbers, peeled and diced

2 cups plain yogurt

2 cloves garlic, pressed

Salt and pepper, to taste

1 teaspoon olive oil

2 tablespoons finely chopped fresh mint, or 2 teaspoons crushed dried mint

Fresh mint sprigs or crushed dried mint for garnish

Pita bread

Put diced cucumbers in a serving bowl. In another bowl, beat the yogurt and garlic together and add salt and pepper to taste. Stir in the mint. Pour the mixture over the cucumber. Mix together. Garnish with sprigs of fresh mint (or sprinkle with crushed dried mint). Drizzle olive oil and serve with pita bread.

Avocado and Olive Salad

1 avocado, peeled, pitted, and sliced

2 cups pitted green olives

3 tablespoons fresh parsley

1 clove garlic, minced or pressed

3 tablespoons olive oil

Coarse salt

Black pepper

Combine the avocado, olives, parsley, and garlic. Drizzle with olive oil. Salt and pepper to taste.

CHICKEN CURRY SALAD WITH TOASTED ALMONDS

5 skinless, boneless chicken breast halves

1 cup mayonnaise

¾ cup chutney

1 teaspoon curry powder

¼ teaspoon black pepper, freshly ground

⅔ cup blanched slivered almonds, toasted

1 cup seedless grapes, halved

½ cup onion, chopped

In a large saucepan, simmer chicken breasts in water for 7 to 10 minutes, or until cooked through. Drain, cool, and pull chicken apart into small pieces, and set aside. Combine mayonnaise, chutney, curry powder, and black pepper in a bowl. Stir in chicken, toasted almonds, grapes, and onions. Cover and chill several hours before serving.

Diced Vegetable and Pomegranate Salad

2 green bell peppers, diced into ½-inch cubes

4 large tomatoes, diced into ½-inch cubes

2 onions, peeled and finely chopped

2 small to medium cucumbers, peeled and diced into ½-inch cubes

2 eggs, hardboiled and diced

¼ cup olive oil

2 tablespoons white wine vinegar

Pinch of coarse salt and freshly ground black pepper

½ pomegranate

Combine first five ingredients in a bowl. To make dressing, combine the olive oil, vinegar, salt, and pepper. Drizzle dressing over salad then toss. Hold the pomegranate over the salad. Using a spatula or spoon, release the seeds and juice over the top of the salad. Chill for at least an hour before serving.

KOSHER BEAN SALAD

1 cup chickpeas

1 cup cucumber, seeded and cubed

2 cups tomatoes, cubed

1 cup yellow, sweet onion, cubed

2 tablespoons red wine vinegar

1 tablespoon olive oil

1 tablespoon basil, finely chopped

1 tablespoon mint, finely chopped

1 tablespoon parsley, finely chopped

Salt and pepper, to taste

Toss all ingredients in large bowl. Chill at least an hour before serving.

Tuna-and-Avocado Salad Pita Pockets

1 (6-ounce) can tuna packed in water, drained

1 medium carrot, chopped

1 stalk celery, chopped

1 bunch radishes, trimmed and sliced

½ cup Monterey Jack cheese cubes

¼ cup frozen green peas, thawed and drained

¼ teaspoon dried parsley flakes

⅓ cup olive oil

1 package pita bread rounds

1 head lettuce, separated into whole leaves

1 medium tomato, sliced

1 avocado, peeled, pitted, and sliced

Place tuna in a bowl and break into chunks with a fork. Fold in chopped carrot, celery, radishes, cheese, peas, and parsley. Drizzle olive oil over tuna salad and toss lightly to coat. Cut pita rounds in half. Insert lettuce leaf, tomato slice, and avocado slice into each pita half. Then fill with tuna salad.

Gorgonzola-and-Olive-Stuffed Grape Leaves

¾ cup green olives, chopped

¾ cup kalamata olives, chopped

½ cup Gorgonzola cheese, crumbled

¾ cup macadamia nuts, chopped

5 tablespoons fresh basil leaves, chopped

4 Roma (plum) tomatoes, seeded and chopped

½ red bell pepper, chopped

½ medium onion, chopped

1 small carrot, peeled and finely diced

3½ tablespoons fresh garlic, chopped

2 tablespoons brown sugar

Salt, to taste

¼ teaspoon ground black pepper

1 (8-ounce) jar grape leaves packed in brine

Combine all ingredients, except for grape leaves, in a large bowl. Lay grape leaves flat. Place a rounded tablespoonful of salad in the center of each grape leaf. Fold or roll the leaf around the salad and place fold-side down in a flat serving dish. Chill, covered, until ready to serve.

Israeli Salad with Pine Nuts

8 Roma (plum) tomatoes, diced

1 English cucumber, peeled and diced

1 cup jicama, peeled and chopped

1 small yellow bell pepper, diced

½ cup red onion, diced

3 tablespoons fresh lemon juice

3 tablespoons extra-virgin olive oil

1 tablespoon dried parsley

Salt and pepper, to taste

½ cup pine nuts

8 ounces feta cheese, crumbled

Toss tomatoes, cucumber, jicama, bell pepper, and red onion in a bowl. Add lemon juice, olive oil, and parsley. Coat vegetables thoroughly. Season with salt and pepper. Garnish with pine nuts and feta cheese. Chill an hour before serving.

LEBANESE FATTOUSH

½ cup water

1 teaspoon cornstarch

⅓ cup lemon juice

2 cloves garlic, minced

2 teaspoons sumac powder

Coarse salt and fresh ground black pepper, to taste

1 head romaine lettuce, torn into bite-sized pieces

1 cup lentil sprouts

1 medium cucumber, diced

½ cup radishes, thinly sliced

2 large tomatoes, diced

4 green onions, chopped

¼ cup chopped fresh flat-leaf parsley

¼ cup fresh mint, chopped

1 green bell pepper, seeded and chopped

1 cup purslane, chopped

½ (5-ounce) package arugula

4–5 pita rounds, toasted and torn into pieces

For dressing, mix water and cornstarch in a small saucepan over medium-high heat until it thickens. Remove from heat and stir in lemon juice, garlic, sumac, salt, and pepper. Place dressing in the refrigerator to cool. Combine all vegetables in a large bowl. Pour cooled dressing over salad and toss to coat well. Serve with toasted pita on the side.

Brown Rice and Feta Lentil Salad

½ cup uncooked brown rice

1 cup water

1 teaspoon chicken bouillon granules

1 cup cooked lentils

1 medium tomato, seeded and diced

⅓ cup green onion, thinly sliced

1 small red pepper, finely diced

2 stalks celery, finely diced

1 tablespoon fresh parsley, minced

2 tablespoons red wine vinegar

1 tablespoon olive oil

2 garlic cloves, minced

1 teaspoon lime juice

1 teaspoon lemon juice

2 teaspoons Dijon mustard

½ teaspoon salt

¼ teaspoon pepper

1 cup (4 ounces) feta cheese, crumbled

Bring rice, water, and bouillon to a boil in a saucepan. Reduce heat; cover and simmer for 40 minutes, or until rice is cooked. Remove from heat and allow rice to cool. Combine rice, lentils, tomato, green onion, red pepper, celery, and parsley. Combine remaining ingredients in a small bowl. Drizzle dressing over the brown rice salad and toss to coat. Top with feta cheese. Cover and refrigerate for at least 1 hour.

4

MAIN COURSES

Ruz Bijajj (Chicken with Rice Pilaf)

1 medium chicken

1 cinnamon stick

1 pound ground beef or veal

1½ cups long-grain rice

1½ teaspoons salt, divided

½ teaspoon black pepper

½ teaspoon allspice

½ cup almonds, blanched

¼ cup pine nuts

3 tablespoons butter, divided

1 tablespoon margarine

Place a stewing chicken in enough water to cover. Bring to boil. Add pepper, 1 teaspoon salt, and a cinnamon stick and simmer chicken until meat comes easily from the bone. Remove meat in large pieces from the bone. Place aside and reserve the stock. Sauté meat (beef or veal) in margarine until cooked. Add ½ teaspoon of salt and allspice. For every 2 cups of stock, take one cup of rice which has been soaked in hot water for half an hour and fry gently in 3 tablespoons butter. Then boil the rice in chicken broth until tender. The broth will be absorbed. Add browned meat and mix together. In a frying pan, sauté almonds and pine nuts until brown, not burned (sauté separately in 1 tablespoon margarine as the pine nuts cook faster). Place aside. To serve, spread cooked rice on a serving platter and cover with the meat mixture. Garnish with the boneless pieces of chicken as desired and add nuts. Serve hot.

Note: May be served with plain yogurt or Cucumber and Yogurt Salad.

Kefta Kabab Siniyeh

2 pounds lean ground beef

1 large onion

½ cup of fresh parsley

Salt, to taste

Pepper, to taste

1 teaspoon paprika

4 medium potatoes, sliced in ½-inch rounds

2 fresh ripe tomatoes, cut in ½-inch rounds

1 small can stewed tomatoes, heated

Finely chop onion and parsley in a food processor. Add onions and parsley to ground beef in a large bowl. Add salt and pepper to taste. Using about ¼ cup mixture for each, form into small balls then flatten into patties. Place meat patties in greased 13x9-inch dish. Cover the meat with potato slices. Sprinkle paprika over potatoes. Cover with foil tent. Bake at 350 degrees for 30 minutes. Uncover. Add the heated stewed tomatoes. Cover with fresh tomatoes and bake for an additional 20 minutes, uncovered, until brown. Or broil for 10 minutes to brown. Serve hot.

LABAN IMMU

1 cup uncooked brown rice

2 cups water

1 teaspoon beef bouillon granules

1 leg or shoulder of lamb or veal, cut in 1-inch cubes

4 onions, sliced

2 tablespoons olive oil

2 cups yogurt

3 tablespoons butter, divided

2 tablespoons flour mixed with 2 tablespoons water

4 fresh sprigs of thyme

1 egg, beaten

1 tablespoon lemon juice

2 cloves garlic, minced

1 teaspoon mint, dried

Salt

Bring rice, water, and bouillon to a boil in a saucepan. Reduce heat; cover and simmer for 40 minutes or until rice is cooked. Remove rice from heat to cool. Brown onions in 2 tablespoons butter in another saucepan. Add the lamb or veal and thyme, and sauté for 5 minutes. Cover with water and bring to a boil. Lower heat and simmer for almost 1 hour or until meat is cooked and tender. In the meantime, combine yogurt, egg, flour, lemon juice, and salt in a saucepan and bring to a boil, stir continually. When it starts to boil, lower heat; add lamb or veal. Simmer for an additional 10 minutes. Heat remaining butter in a small skillet; add garlic, and mint, sauté for several minutes. Pour garlic mixture over the yogurt and lamb. Serve on a bed of brown rice.

Halibut with Mediterranean Salsa

4 (6-ounce) lean mild fish fillets, such as halibut, flounder, tilapia, or snapper

2 tablespoons water

½ teaspoon chili powder

1 teaspoon dried thyme

1 teaspoon freshly graded lemon zest

1 large tomato, seeded and chopped

1 (2½-ounce) can sliced ripe olives or kalamata olives, drained

2 tablespoons chopped fresh parsley

1 tablespoons lemon juice

1 tablespoon capers, drained

2 teaspoons extra-virgin olive oil

1 teaspoon dried oregano

Preheat oven to 350 degrees. Coat baking dish with nonstick cooking spray; arrange fillets in a single layer. Pour water over fish. Sprinkle with chili powder, thyme, and lemon zest. Cover dish with aluminum foil. Bake 15 minutes, or until fish flakes easily. For the salsa, combine chopped tomato, olives, parsley, lemon juice, capers, oil, and oregano in a bowl, and mix well. To serve, remove fish from the baking dish and place on serving platter. Top with salsa.

Healthy Black Bean Burger

½ onion, diced

1 tablespoon extra-virgin olive oil

1 (15-ounce) can black beans

½ cup flour

2 slices bread, crumbled

1 teaspoon garlic powder

1 teaspoon onion powder

Salt and pepper, to taste

Whole grain buns

½ head lettuce, separated into leaves

Tomato, sliced

Pickles, sliced

Purple onion, sliced

Mustard

Sautee onions in olive oil 3 to 5 minutes. Mash beans until almost smooth in a large bowl. Add sautéed onions, crumbled bread, garlic powder, and onion powder. Add flour, a few tablespoons at a time, and combine well. Mixture will be thick. Form black bean mixture into patties. Cook over medium heat in a pan that is lightly covered with extra-virgin olive oil. Salt and pepper to taste. Cook until both sides are lightly browned. Serve on whole grain buns with lettuce, tomato, pickles, onions, and mustard.

Greek Isles Asparagus Omelet

2 tablespoons olive oil, divided

¼ cup onion, diced

¼ cup wild green asparagus, chopped

¼ cup canned artichoke hearts, rinsed and drained

¼ cup spinach leaves, washed and torn

¼ cup Roma (plum) tomatoes, diced

2 tablespoons pitted ripe olives, sliced

9 eggs

Salt, to taste

Black pepper, to taste

Sauté onions in 1 tablespoon olive oil over medium heat until translucent and tender. Add asparagus and artichoke hearts. Sauté until heated through. Add spinach, tomatoes, and olives, and continue to sauté. Remove vegetables from heat and transfer to a bowl. Combine eggs, salt, and black pepper in another bowl. Heat remaining olive oil in a skillet over medium heat until hot. Pour eggs into skillet. Cook 5 to 7 minutes or until eggs are cooked nearly through. Spoon vegetables over half of eggs. Loosen omelet with spatula, fold in half over vegetables and slide onto a serving plate.

Main Dish Mediterranean Tuna Salad

1 (10-ounce) package ready-to-serve chopped romaine lettuce

1 (5½-ounce) pouch solid white tuna, flaked

2 hard boiled eggs, diced

½ pound fresh green beans, cooked and drained

1 (8-ounce) carton cherry tomatoes, quartered

¼ cup green pepper, finely chopped

3 tablespoons olive oil

2 tablespoons rice vinegar or apple cider vinegar

1½ teaspoons Dijon mustard

½ teaspoon black pepper

Combine lettuce, tuna, eggs, green beans, tomatoes, and green peppers in salad bowl. For dressing, whisk oil, vinegar, mustard, and pepper in a small bowl. Drizzle dressing over salad and toss well. Spoon salad onto plates to serve.

Apple-Turkey Gyros

1 tablespoon vegetable oil

1 cup onion, sliced thin

½ cup cucumber, sliced thin

½ cup red bell pepper, sliced thin

½ cup green bell pepper, sliced thin

1 teaspoon dried dill weed

2 tablespoons lemon juice

½ pound turkey breast, cut into thin strips

1 medium apple, cored and thinly sliced

6 pita bread rounds, lightly toasted and halved

½ cup plain yogurt

½ cup feta cheese, crumbled

Sauté onion, cucumber, and peppers in olive oil until tender. Add dill weed and lemon juice. Add turkey and cook until heated through. Remove from heat and add apple. Fill each pita half with apple turkey mixture. Drizzle with yogurt and top with crumbled feta.

CHICKEN JERUSALEM WITH EGGPLANT

4 skinless, boneless chicken breast halves

2 cups chicken broth

2 cloves garlic, crushed

½ small onion, finely chopped

1 cup white wine

1 large eggplant, peeled and cut lengthwise

1 (8-ounce) package sliced fresh mushrooms

1 (10-ounce) can artichoke hearts, drained

1 cup heavy cream

1 tablespoon fresh basil, finely chopped

Coarse salt and fresh ground black pepper, to taste

Preheat oven to 325 degrees. Place chicken in a 9x13-inch baking dish. Bake for 25 to 30 minutes, or until chicken is no longer pink and juices run clear. While the chicken is baking, place the chicken stock, garlic, and onion in a medium saucepan. Bring the broth to a boil and cook until liquid is reduced by half. Stir in wine, and continue to cook until reduced and slightly thickened. Next add eggplant, mushrooms, and artichokes to the sauce. Reduce heat, and simmer until vegetables are tender. Stir in the heavy cream and basil. Cook, stirring occasionally, until thick. Season with salt and pepper. Pour the sauce over the chicken to serve.

MIDDLE EASTERN RICE AND BEANS

2 tablespoons olive oil, divided

1 medium onion, finely chopped

1 clove garlic, minced

1 cup basmati rice, uncooked

2 teaspoons ground cumin

2 teaspoons ground coriander

1 teaspoon ground turmeric

1 teaspoon ground cayenne pepper

1 quart lamb or vegetable stock

1½ pounds ground lamb

2 (15-ounce) cans chickpeas, drained and rinsed

2 (15-ounce) cans black beans, drained and rinsed

1 tablespoon lime juice

1 bunch fresh cilantro, chopped

1 bunch fresh parsley, chopped

¼ cup pine nuts

Coarse salt and fresh ground black pepper, to taste

Heat olive oil in a large saucepan. Sauté onion and garlic until tender. Add rice, cumin, coriander, turmeric, and cayenne pepper. Cook 5 to 7 minutes, stirring constantly. Add lamb or vegetable stock and bring to a boil. Reduce heat to low, cover, and simmer 20 minutes. Sauté lamb in remaining olive oil in a skillet over medium heat until evenly browned. Combine lamb, chickpeas, black beans, lemon juice, cilantro, parsley, and pine nuts with the cooked rice. Salt and pepper to taste.

Kingdom Kabobs

2 pounds beef sirloin or tenderloin, cut into 1-inch cubes

4 limes, sliced

½ cup olive oil

1 tablespoon white vinegar

1 teaspoon cumin

½ teaspoon coriander

½ teaspoon paprika

1 teaspoon garlic, minced

The day before grilling, prepare marinade by combining olive oil, vinegar, cumin, coriander, paprika, and garlic. Place beef cubes in a sealable storage dish and pour marinade over beef cubes. Seal and place in refrigerator, allowing beef to marinate overnight.

When ready to grill, spray skewers and grill with nonstick spray. Remove beef from the refrigerator. Thread meat and sliced limes onto skewers. Grill meat on each side until done. Depending on the heat of your grill and desired doneness of the meat, grill 3 to 4 minutes per side, or 8 minutes altogether. Serve with dipping sauce, pita bread, or over a bed of rice. You may also add vegetables such as cherry tomatoes, onions, potatoes, bell peppers, eggplant, zucchini, or squash to the kabobs.

5

VEGETABLES

Cauliflower, Potato, and Onion Latkes

1 cup cauliflower florets

1½ cups mashed potatoes

½ cup onion, finely chopped

3 tablespoons matzoh meal

2 teaspoons garlic, minced

1 teaspoon salt

1 egg, beaten

2 tablespoons kasha

5 tablespoons extra-virgin olive oil

Place cauliflower in a large pot of boiling water. Cook 12 to15 minutes until tender. Mash cooked cauliflower in a bowl. Stir in mashed potatoes, onion, matzoh meal, garlic, salt, and egg. Blend thoroughly. Shape into patties. Sprinkle kasha onto patties, press into both sides. Heat olive oil in a skillet. Sauté latkes over medium heat, until golden brown and crisp. Cool on paper towels before serving.

Roasted Asparagus

1 pound fresh asparagus, washed and trimmed

3 tablespoons extra-virgin olive oil

½ teaspoon kosher salt

Preheat oven to 375 degrees. Place asparagus on nonstick baking sheet. Drizzle olive oil and kosher salt over asparagus. Roast 15 to 18 minutes until tender. Move to platter to serve.

ROASTED EGGPLANT WITH ONIONS AND MUSHROOMS

2 medium eggplants, sliced

½ medium yellow onion, chopped

1 (8-ounce) package mushrooms, sliced

2 tablespoons tomato paste

½ cup water

1 clove garlic, minced

¼ teaspoon dried oregano

¼ teaspoon dried basil

Pinch of salt and pepper

Preheat oven to 450 degrees. Place eggplant, onion, and mushrooms in a nonstick casserole dish. In a small bowl combine the tomato paste, water, garlic, oregano, basil, salt, and pepper. Pour over the eggplant vegetable dish. Bake in preheated oven for 30 to 40 minutes, or until eggplant is tender. Add water as necessary if vegetables begin to stick. Vegetables should be slightly dry, with browned edges.

Roasted Root Vegetables

2 cups pearl onions, boiled and peeled

2 pounds red potatoes cut into ½-inch pieces

1 large turnip, peeled and cubed

1 large rutabaga, peeled and cut into ½ inch pieces

1 pound parsnips, peeled and cut into ½ inch pieces

1 pound carrots, cut into ½ inch pieces

6 tablespoons olive oil

1 tablespoon red wine vinegar

4 teaspoons dried thyme

½ teaspoon dried rosemary

1½ teaspoons salt

¾ teaspoon coarsely ground pepper

2 (10-ounce) packages frozen Brussels sprouts, thawed

3 cloves garlic, minced

Place onions, potatoes, turnip, rutabaga, parsnips, and carrots in a large nonstick roasting pan. Drizzle with olive oil. Sprinkle with thyme, rosemary, salt, and pepper; toss to coat. Bake covered at 425 degrees for 30 minutes. Stir in Brussels sprouts, garlic, and red wine vinegar. Bake, uncovered, for 50 to 60 minutes or until vegetables are tender and begin to brown.

MIDDLE EASTERN VEGGIE WRAP

1 large eggplant, thinly sliced lengthwise

¾ pound mushrooms, thinly sliced

½ red bell pepper, sliced lengthwise

½ green bell pepper, sliced lengthwise

½ zucchini, thinly sliced lengthwise

6 tablespoons extra-virgin olive oil

2 green onions, chopped

⅛ cup fresh lemon juice

⅛ cup fresh lime juice

⅛ teaspoon black pepper

1 package flour tortillas

½ cup store-bought hummus

⅓ cup fresh cilantro, finely chopped

6 fresh basil leaves, crumbled

6 fresh mint leaves, crumbled

4 tablespoons feta cheese, crumbled

Preheat oven to 375 degrees. Place all vegetables except green onions on nonstick baking sheet. Drizzle olive oil over top. Roast 15 minutes. Meanwhile, combine green onions, lemon and lime juice, and black pepper in medium bowl. Add roasted vegetables to this mixture. Combine basil, cilantro, and mint. Lay out tortillas. Layer hummus, herbs, and vegetables down the center of each tortilla. Sprinkle feta cheese on top. Roll up, creating the veggie wrap. Serve warm.

GREEK STUFFED EGGPLANT

1 large eggplant, halved lengthwise, pulped: save pulp for recipe

2 tablespoons extra-virgin olive oil

½ cup onion, finely chopped

1 clove garlic, minced

2 tablespoons margarine, melted

2 tablespoons flour

1 pound canned diced tomatoes; reserve juice

½ cup water

¼ teaspoon dried oregano

¼ teaspoon marjoram

¼ teaspoon fresh black pepper

Coarse salt, to taste

½ cup cheese, crumbled feta or drained cottage cheese

Preheat oven to 350 degrees. Microwave eggplant shell for 7 to 8 minutes on high in a 13x9-inch dish, until tender. Heat olive oil in skillet over medium heat. Chop eggplant pulp and sauté in oil along with onion and garlic until tender. Add melted margarine, flour, juice from tomatoes, and water to skillet. Cook, stirring, until thick. Add tomatoes, oregano, marjoram, pepper, and salt. Sauté for an additional 5 minutes, until heated through. Spoon stuffing into eggplant shells. Sprinkle with cheese. Bake stuffed eggplant at 350 degrees for 30 minutes.

Couscous-Stuffed Peppers

1 cup dehydrated sun-dried tomatoes

1½ cups water

½ (10-ounce) package couscous

1 teaspoon olive oil

3 cloves garlic, pressed

1 bunch green onions, chopped

⅓ cup fresh basil leaves

¼ cup fresh cilantro, chopped

1 tablespoon lemon juice

1 tablespoon lime juice

Salt and pepper, to taste

4 ounces Portobello mushroom caps, sliced

4 green bell peppers, capped, seeded, and rinsed

1 package feta cheese, crumbled

Preheat oven to 350 degrees. Spray baking sheet with nonstick cooking spray. Place sun-dried tomatoes in a bowl with 1 cup water. Soak 30 minutes, until rehydrated. Drain, reserving water, and chop. In a medium saucepan, combine the reserved sun-dried tomato water with enough water to yield 1½ cups. Bring to a boil. Stir in couscous. Cover and remove from heat, allowing liquid to be absorbed; then fluff with a fork. Heat olive oil in skillet. Add sun-dried tomatoes, garlic, and green onions. Sauté until green onions are tender. Add basil, cilantro, lemon and lime juice. Season with salt and pepper. Mix in mushrooms; sauté an additional 3 minutes. Toss sun-dried tomatoes with green onion and mushroom mixture and couscous. Spoon couscous mixture into bell peppers and place peppers upright on baking sheet. Sprinkle peppers with crumbled feta cheese. Bake at 350 degrees for approximately 20 minutes. Serve warm.

ISRAELI PLATTER WITH FRESH FALAFEL

2 tablespoons fresh lemon juice

1 tablespoon fresh lime juice

2 tablespoons extra-virgin olive oil

4 plum tomatoes, seeded and diced

1 cucumber, seeded and diced

1 cup parsley, coarsely chopped

1 small red onion, diced

½ teaspoon ground cumin

½ teaspoon ground coriander

Kosher salt

Fresh ground black pepper

1 container hummus

½ teaspoon paprika

8 ounces feta cheese, sliced thick

1 cup pitted kalamata olives

Flatbread, torn into pieces

Falafel

1 cup dried chickpeas

2 tablespoons bulgur

2 cloves garlic, minced

4 onions, coarsely chopped

3 tablespoons parsley, chopped

1 teaspoon ground coriander

1 teaspoon ground cumin

¼ teaspoon cayenne pepper

1 tablespoon lemon juice

1½ teaspoons salt freshly ground black pepper

½ teaspoon soda

Vegetable oil, for sautéing

Combine lemon and lime juice with 1 tablespoon olive oil in a bowl. Combine tomatoes, cucumber, onions, parsley, ground cumin, and coriander in another bowl. Drizzle olive oil dressing over the vegetables. Season to taste with salt and pepper. Toss to combine. Place vegetable salad on Israeli platter. Sprinkle hummus with paprika and remaining olive oil. Top with feta slices and olives. Spoon hummus onto the Israeli platter. Place flatbread pieces on the platter beside hummus.

For falafel, place chickpeas in a large bowl and cover with cold water. Soak in the refrigerator overnight. Drain and place in pan with fresh water. Bring to a boil, then simmer for 1 hour. Drain. Place bulgur in a sieve and rinse. Transfer to bowl, cover, and let stand until it softens, approximately 20 minutes. Place drained chickpeas, bulgur, and the remaining ingredients in a food processor and blend until pastelike. Cover and let stand for 30 minutes. Shape tablespoons of the mixture into thick 1½ inch patties. Heat the oil for cooking to 375 degrees. Sauté falafel patties about 5 minutes, until evenly browned throughout (including the middle). Drain on paper towel. Serve falafel on platter alongside vegetable salad, hummus, and flatbread.

SPINACH-STUFFED SHELLS

1 package fresh spinach, washed and finely chopped

1½ cups ricotta cheese

½ cup grated Parmesan cheese

5 eggs

3 cloves garlic, finely chopped

1 teaspoon dried oregano

½ teaspoon salt

½ teaspoon dried basil

½ teaspoon dried marjoram

¼ teaspoon fresh ground black pepper

24 cooked large pasta shells

2 (14-ounce) cans crushed tomatoes, undrained

1 cup mozzarella cheese, shredded

Preheat oven to 350 degrees. Spray baking dish with nonstick cooking spray. Combine spinach, ricotta, Parmesan, garlic, herbs, eggs, and seasonings in large bowl. Spoon mixture into pasta shells and place in baking dish. Top stuffed shells with tomatoes, juice, and mozzarella. Bake, covered, for 20 minutes.

VEGETABLE MEDLEY

2 large carrots, peeled and sliced

1 small head broccoli, chopped

½ cup cauliflower, chopped

1 large zucchini, sliced

1 cup apple juice

1 teaspoon caraway seeds

1 tablespoon extra-virgin olive oil

¼ teaspoon salt

½ cup slivered almonds

Place all ingredients in large cooking pot. Add olive oil and salt. Cover; heat to boiling. Reduce heat and simmer on low for 18 to 20 minutes. Arrange vegetables on serving platter. Sprinkle with slivered almonds.

Cucumber Drink

1 large cucumber, peeled and chopped

2 cups water

1 cup ice

3 tablespoons sugar, or to taste

2 tablespoons lemon juice, or to taste

2 tablespoons lime juice, or to taste

Place cucumber in blender. Puree with other ingredients until smooth. Serve cold. Garnish side of glass with sliced lemon and lime.

BAKED ARTICHOKE CASSEROLE

2 medium fresh artichokes

2 tablespoons lemon juice

2 medium onions, thickly sliced

2 tablespoons olive oil

½ teaspoon curry powder

¾ teaspoon ground cumin

½ teaspoon garlic salt

2 medium tomatoes, sliced

6 ounces mozzarella or Monterey Jack cheese, sliced

Bend back outer petals of each artichoke until they snap off easily near base. Edible portion of petals should remain on artichoke bottom. Continue to snap off and discard thick petals until central core of pale green petals is reached. Trim brown end of stem and cut off top 2 inches of artichokes; discard. Pare outer dark green surface layer from bottom. Cut out center petals and fuzzy centers. Slice artichoke bottoms about ¼-inch slices. Toss artichoke slices with lemon juice to prevent discoloration; set aside. Sauté onions 5 to 8 minutes in olive oil, until tender; spoon evenly into baking dish. Arrange tomato and artichoke slices over onions. Sprinkle with curry powder, ground cumin, and garlic salt. Cover with cheese slices. Cook, covered, in 375-degree oven for 35 to 40 minutes.

Eggs with Tomatoes

1 tablespoon olive oil

5 large fresh tomatoes, coarsely chopped

1 tablespoon minced garlic

1 teaspoon ground cumin

1 teaspoon coarse salt, or to taste

6 eggs

4 pita bread rounds, halved

Heat olive oil in a large nonstick skillet, over medium-high heat. Add chopped tomatoes, garlic, cumin, and salt. Stir occasionally until liquid cooks out of tomatoes. Carefully break eggs over tomatoes, without breaking yolks. Lightly season with salt, reduce heat, and cover. Simmer covered for 20 minutes, or until yolks are fully cooked. Add more salt as needed. Spoon into warm pita pockets.

ROASTED RED BELL PEPPERS AND TOMATOES WITH MINT AND YOGURT

2 ounces plain yogurt

3 red bell peppers, sliced

3 tomatoes, sliced

3 tablespoons extra-virgin olive oil

¼ cup pecans, coarsely chopped

2 tablespoons mint, finely chopped

Coarse salt, to taste,

Freshly ground black pepper, to taste

Pita bread, warmed

Preheat oven to 375 degrees. Place red pepper and tomato slices on a nonstick baking sheet. Drizzle with olive oil. Roast 15 to18 minutes. Meanwhile, spread a thick layer of yogurt in a serving dish, or on individual plates. Place roasted peppers and tomatoes over the yogurt. Sprinkle with pecans and mint. Add salt and pepper to taste. Serve with warm pita bread.

6

BREADS,
SPREADS, AND
SAUCES

Krugel Bread

¾ pound challah, broken in pieces, soaked in hot water, drained

4 eggs, beaten

½ cup golden raisins

3 small apples, peeled, finely chopped

½ teaspoon baking powder

1 teaspoon cinnamon

1 cup sugar

½ teaspoon nutmeg

1 teaspoon vanilla

¼ cup walnuts, chopped

¼ cup almonds, slivered

Preheat oven to 350 degrees. Mix together challah, eggs, raisins, apples, and baking powder. Pour into nonstick baking dish sprayed with nonstick spray. In a small bowl, mix together cinnamon, sugar, nutmeg, and vanilla. Sprinkle cinnamon mixture over krugel bread. Top with nuts. Bake for 45 minutes.

SPINACH CHEESE BOURIKAS

3 tablespoons extra-virgin olive oil

1 onion, finely chopped

1 (10-ounce) package frozen chopped spinach, thawed, drained, and squeezed dry

1 teaspoon coarse salt

⅛ teaspoon freshly ground black pepper

1 (4-ounce) package feta cheese, crumbled

½ cup cottage cheese

1 egg, beaten

1 (16-ounce) package phyllo dough

1 cup unsalted butter, melted

2 tablespoons sesame seeds

Preheat oven to 400 degrees. Heat olive oil in a medium saucepan over medium heat. Sauté onion until translucent and tender. Add spinach, salt, and pepper. Add feta cheese, cottage cheese, and egg. Cook 5 to10 minutes, or until thick. Reduce heat to simmer. Unroll phyllo dough sheets, one at a time. Brush with melted butter. Cut into 4½- to 5-inch strips. Spoon 1 tablespoon of spinach mixture at one end of each phyllo strip. Fold the end of the strip over the filling to make a triangle. Continue folding the phyllo dough strip until a small, triangular stuffed pastry is made. Brush top of triangle with melted butter and place on a nonstick baking sheet. Repeat the process until all the dough and spinach mixture are used. Continue placing triangles on backing sheet, allowing room for each to expand slightly. Sprinkle with sesame seeds to garnish. Bake in preheated oven 12 to15 minutes, until flaky and golden brown. Serve warm.

BABA GHANNOUJ (EGGPLANT/AUBERGINE SPREAD)

1 large eggplant

2 cloves garlic, minced or pressed

¼–½ cup lemon juice, to taste

¼ cup, or 4 tablespoons, tahini (sesame paste)

1 teaspoon salt

3–4 teaspoons olive oil

Garnish

2 tablespoons lemon juice

2 teaspoons olive oil

Preheat oven to 375 degrees. Pierce eggplant in several places with a fork. Place on a baking sheet and bake for 30 minutes, or until outside is crisp and inside is soft. Allow to cool for 20 minutes. Cut open eggplant and scoop out the flesh into a colander and allow to drain for 10 minutes. Removing excess liquid helps to eliminate a bitter flavor. Place eggplant flesh in a medium-sized bowl; add remaining ingredients and mash together or puree in a food processor. Pulse for about 2 minutes. Place in serving bowl and top with lemon juice and olive oil mixture. Add other garnishments according to taste. Serve as a spread on warm or toasted pita or flatbread.

Garnishing Options

Baba ghannouj must always be garnished with olive oil. To spice things up, add crushed red pepper, a dash of cumin, and/or parsley.

Note: If making ahead, refrigerate in a sealed container. Bring to room temperature before serving.

Honey Feta Spread

1 (4-ounce) package feta cheese

1 cup sweet, wild honey

3 tablespoons cracked black peppercorns

2 sprigs fresh clover

Crackers

Place feta in the center of serving plate. Drizzle with honey. Sprinkle cracked black pepper over feta and honey. Arrange crackers around sides of serving dish. Garnish with fresh clover. Spread on crackers.

THREE-OLIVE SPREAD

1 cup black olives, pitted

1 cup green olives, pitted

1 cup kalamata olives, pitted

1–2 cloves garlic, peeled and minced

1 green onion, finely chopped

3 tablespoons balsamic vinegar

3 tablespoons extra-virgin olive oil

⅛ teaspoon freshly ground black pepper

Crackers

Combine black olives, green olives, kalamata olives, and garlic in food processor. Pulse to chop. Add balsamic vinegar, extra-virgin olive oil, and black pepper. Process until smooth. Spoon spread into serving bowl. Top with green onion. Refrigerate to chill. Serve with crackers.

SUN-DRIED TOMATO BREAKFAST SPREAD

2 (6-ounce) cans tomato paste

1½ fresh basil leaves, finely chopped

¼ cup extra-virgin olive oil

1 teaspoon garlic, minced

1 teaspoon lemon juice

¼ cup pine nuts

¾ cup sun-dried tomatoes, packed in oil, drained

½ teaspoon coarse salt

½ teaspoon freshly ground black pepper

1 teaspoon sugar

1 teaspoon garlic salt

Pureé all ingredients in a blender. Mix to the consistency of a spread. Chill in the refrigerator until ready to serve on your favorite bagels, toast, or breakfast bread.

TOMATO WITH MUSHROOM SAUCE

1 large celery stalk, cut into small pieces

1 small onion, chopped

¼ cup green onions, finely chopped

1 green pepper, chopped

1½ pounds mushrooms, sliced

1 (46-ounce) can tomato juice

⅛ teaspoon salt

⅛ teaspoon freshly ground black pepper

Place all ingredients except tomato juice in a medium-hot skillet. Sauté ingredients till tender. Reduce heat and add tomato juice. Simmer over low heat for 50 to 60 minutes. Serve sauce over rice, chicken, beef, or fish.

Kosher Fish or Chicken Sauce

2 stalks celery, diced

2 large carrots, sliced

1 medium onion, finely chopped

1 green pepper, finely chopped

1 can tomato soup

2 medium tomatoes, finely chopped

⅓ cup water

⅛ teaspoon salt

⅛ teaspoon pepper

⅛ teaspoon onion powder, or to taste

Sauté celery, carrots, onion, and green pepper over medium heat until tender. Place tomato soup, tomatoes, water, salt, pepper, and onion powder in medium-to-large sauce pan and bring to slow boil. Reduce heat. Add sautéed vegetables to tomato base, and simmer all ingredients on low for 35 to 40 minutes. Ladle over fish or chicken.

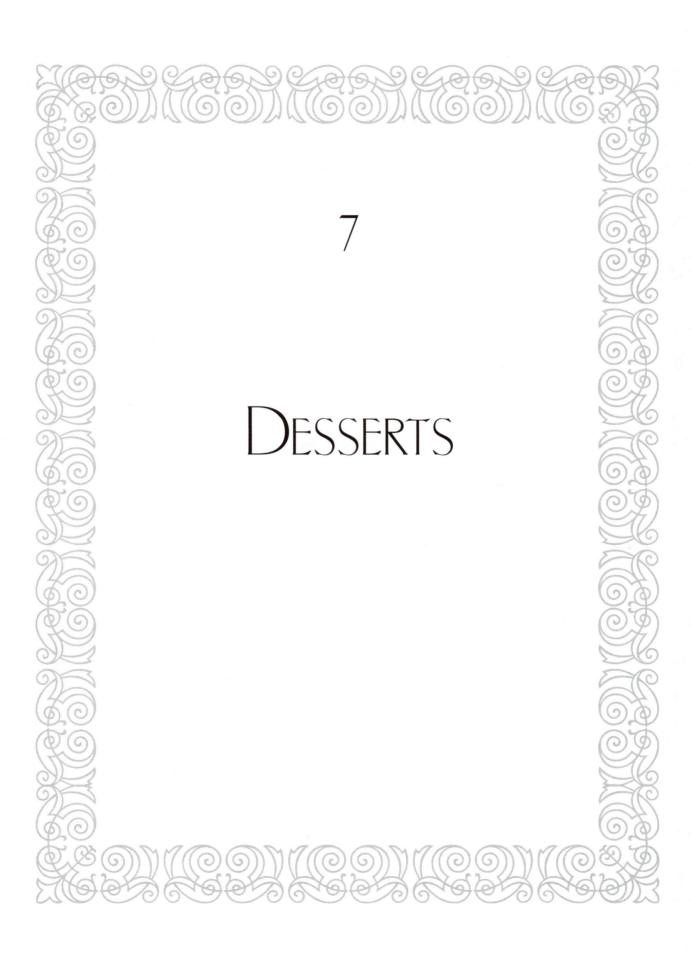

7

DESSERTS

Baklava (Baklawa)

2 cups walnuts or pistachio nuts, coarsely chopped

⅓ cup sugar

1 tablespoon rose water

1 pound phyllo pastry sheets

1 pound sweet butter, melted

Combine nuts, sugar, and rose water. Keep sheets covered at all times with towel to prevent drying out. Spread phyllo pastry dough in a buttered 10x14-inch pan, brushing each layer with butter. Halfway through the layering, place nut mixture in a ½- to ¾-inch layer. Then continue layering buttered phyllo on top. Cut in diamond or square-shaped pieces. Bake at 300 degrees for one hour or until golden brown. Pour cooled syrup over hot baklava using a spouted pot, making sure the syrup is poured in the cracks and around the edges of the pan (keeping it crunchy) and the pastry is well saturated.

Basic Syrup Recipe

2 cups sugar

1 cup water

Few drops of fresh lemon juice

1 teaspoon rose water

Combine sugar, water, and lemon juice in saucepan. Boil over medium heat for 10 to 15 minutes. Before removing from heat, add rose water and let come to a boil. Remove from stove and let cool.

Note: Pour over cold baklava. Or pour cold syrup over hot baklava. If you pour hot syrup over hot baklava, the pastry will turn soggy immediately.

Ghrybeh (Butter Cookies)

2 cups (4 sticks) butter

1 cup superfine sugar

1 cup confectioner's sugar

4 cups (approx.) cake flour

Blanched almond halves

Place butter in mixing bowl and beat with electric mixer for about 10 to 15 minutes until butter is white and fluffy. Add granulated and confectioner's sugar. Whip again thoroughly with a spatula; gradually add flour and continue to mix with spatula until the flour is absorbed and a medium soft dough is formed. Be sure to mix with spatula, because heat from hands melts the butter. Add more flour if needed. Remove mixture to lightly floured surface and quickly roll with floured hands into rope shape about 1½-inch diameter. Cut into 1½-inch pieces on the diagonal forming a diamond or round shape. Place one almond in middle of each diamond. Place on baking sheet at 300 degrees about 10 to 12 minutes, until cookies are set. They should remain white not browned. Let cool on sheet. When cold, remove carefully.

Arabic Honey Cake

4 eggs

2 cups sugar

½ cup oil

½ cup shortening

2 teaspoons baking soda dissolved in 1 cup strong coffee

2 cups honey

7 cups sifted flour

1½ teaspoons baking powder

½ teaspoon salt

1 teaspoon ground ginger

1 teaspoon ground cloves

1 teaspoon cinnamon

½ teaspoon nutmeg

1 (8-ounce) can crushed pineapple

¼ cup butter, warmed

¼ cup honey, warmed

Preheat oven to 325 degrees. Grease 3 loaf pans and line bottom with waxed paper. Beat eggs and sugar together. Add oil, shortening, coffee mixture, and honey. Mix well and set aside. Sift flour, baking powder, salt, ginger, cloves, cinnamon, and nutmeg together. Add to honey mixture. Add crushed pineapple. Place batter into loaf pans. Bake 1 hour, or until thoroughly cooked. Allow time to cool. Pour butter and honey over the cake while hot. Serve with additional bowl of warmed butter and honey for dipping if desired.

JEWISH APPLE CAKE

4 eggs

1 cup sugar plus 3 tablespoons, divided

3 tablespoons lemon juice

1 cup flour

4 red apples, peeled, cored, sliced, brushed with butter

3 green apples, peeled, cored, sliced, brushed with butter

2–3 tablespoons butter, melted

⅛ teaspoon nutmeg

1½ teaspoons cinnamon

Preheat oven to 350 degrees. Grease a 9x11-inch pan or springform pan; dust with flour. Beat egg yolks with 1 cup sugar until light and creamy. Add lemon juice and flour; beat well. Set aside. Pour half the batter into the baking pan. Spread half the apple slices evenly over cake batter. Combine nutmeg and half the cinnamon and 1½ tablespoons sugar mixture over the apples and cake. Pour remaining cake batter over apple layer. Arrange remaining apple slices on top of cake batter. Sprinkle remaining cinnamon and sugar on top. Bake 55 to 65 minutes. Cool slightly and serve warm.

Green Tea Cake

4 eggs

½ cup sugar

⅓ cup flour

2 tablespoons cornstarch

1 tablespoon powdered green tea

⅛ teaspoon cream of tartar

2 tablespoons powdered sugar

Preheat oven to 450 degrees. Spray an 8-inch square pan with nonstick cooking spray. Beat eggs and sugar together until thick. Sift together flour, cornstarch, and green tea. Add to egg and sugar mixture. Add cream of tartar. Pour batter into pan. Bake until light brown. Sprinkle powdered sugar on top.

Dried-Fruit Strudel

6 sheets phyllo pastry

6 ounces butter, melted

⅛ cup tablespoons raisins

⅛ cup dried dates, finely chopped

⅛ cup dried apricots, finely chopped

⅛ cup dried cranberries, finely chopped

2 dried dessert figs, finely chopped

3 tablespoons walnuts, finely chopped

½ lemon rind, freshly grated

½ lime rind, freshly grated

2 tablespoons superfine sugar

¼ teaspoon ground cinnamon

¼ teaspoon ground nutmeg

3 tablespoons soft white breadcrumbs

3 tablespoons almonds, ground

¼ cup sweet wild honey

Preheat oven to 350 degrees. Combine raisins, dates, apricots, cranberries, figs, and walnuts in a bowl. In another bowl, combine lemon and lime zest with sugar, cinnamon, and nutmeg. Brush both sides of each phyllo sheet with melted butter and layer. Sprinkle breadcrumbs over the stack. Top with layer of almonds, drizzle with melted butter. Spread dried fruit and nut mixture evenly on top of phyllo and breadcrumbs. Sprinkle sugar mixture evenly over dried fruit filling. Drizzle with remaining melted butter. Turn the end of the pastry over the filling, and fold in the sides. Brush the side folds with butter. Roll strudel firmly. Place fold-side down on a greased nonstick baking sheet. Using a sharp knife, cut shallow diagonal slashes on top of strudel. Bake 30 to 35 minutes, or until golden brown. Cool, then place on serving plate. Drizzle with honey.

Cinnamon and Almond Jerusalem Pudding

¾ cup cold water, divided

2 tablespoons uncooked rice

1 cup whipping cream

20 dates, pitted and chopped

½ cup powdered sugar

1 teaspoon ground cinnamon

1 envelope unflavored gelatin

½ teaspoon vanilla extract

3½ ounces blanched almonds, finely ground

Bring ½ cup water to a boil in a saucepan. Add rice and stir. Reduce heat, cover, and simmer until rice is cooked. Spread on a plate to cool. Whip the cream until stiff. Stir in the cooled rice, dates, powdered sugar, and cinnamon. Add ¼ cup water to a small saucepan. Sprinkle gelatin over the surface of the water, then set over a large pot of boiling water until gelatin dissolves. Stir into rice mixture and almonds. Add vanilla. Refrigerate until the mixture begins to thicken and pudding is set.

Arabic Rosewater Shortbread Cookies

1 cup pure ghee

1 cup powdered sugar

1 tablespoon rose water

2 cups flour

½ teaspoon baking soda

1 small package pistachios

Preheat oven to 350 degrees. Melt ghee in a saucepan on the stove. Add powdered sugar to ghee and mix till sugar is completely dissolved. Remove from heat. Add rosewater. Stir in flour and baking soda and mix well. If dough is sticky to touch, add more flour. Roll a spoonful of dough at a time into balls. Place on greased baking sheet, flattening tops. Place one pistachio in the center of each dough ball. Bake cookies for 10 minutes, being careful not to brown.

Ghee

To make ghee, melt 2 cups butter in a heavy saucepan. Turn down heat till it just boils. Continue to cook at this heat, uncovered, until clear and no longer sputtering. Take off heat and let cool until just warm. Pour through a sieve and discard curds.

LEBANESE RICE PUDDING

¾ cup rice

1 cup sugar

1 quart whole milk

2 tablespoons vanilla

¼ teaspoon lemon juice

Orange marmalade

Cook the rice according to package directions. Add sugar and milk to cooked rice and mix thoroughly. Continue cooking on low for 5 to 6 minutes. Remove pudding from heat. Stir in vanilla and lemon juice. When cool, spoon into cups and top with a spoonful of orange marmalade.

Pistachio and Almond Fruit Balls

¾ cup roasted pistachios, finely chopped, divided, saving ¼ cup for coating

½ cup walnuts, finely chopped

½ cup dried cranberries, finely chopped

½ cup dried cherries, finely chopped

½ cup dried apricots, finely chopped

½ cup golden raisins, finely chopped

½ cup pitted dates, ground

1 tablespoon orange juice

2 tablespoons crème de cassis

Mix nuts and dried fruits together. Add orange juice and crème de cassis. Mix thoroughly with hands and form into balls. Roll in pistachios to coat. Store tightly covered.

DATES WITH BANANAS

1 cup heavy whipping cream

1½ tablespoons pure wild honey

1 cup whole dates, pitted and thinly sliced

3 large ripe bananas, sliced

1 teaspoon ground cinnamon

¼ teaspoon ground nutmeg

Beat whipping cream and honey with mixer. Fold in bananas and dates. Sprinkle with cinnamon and nutmeg. Cover and chill for one hour before serving.

Hamantashen

3 eggs

1 cup honey

¾ cup orange juice

½ cup oil

3 teaspoons baking powder

5 cups flour

1 tablespoon orange zest

12 ounces pastry filling

½ cup raisins, ground

½ teaspoon lemon juice

¼ cup almonds, chopped

¼ cup walnuts, chopped

1 egg, beaten and thinned with water

Combine eggs, honey, orange juice, oil, baking powder, flour, and orange zest, mixing dough well. Refrigerate overnight. Preheat oven to 350 degrees.

For pastry filling, combine raisins, lemon juice, almonds, and walnuts. Roll dough flat. Cut into 2-inch squares. Place teaspoon of filling in center of dough square. Close top, pinching dough at three corners to create triangles and place on a greased cookie sheet. Brush triangular, hamantashen pastries with thinned egg mixture. Bake until pastries are light brown.

Baked Shabbat Carrot-Raisin Pudding

12 tablespoons butter, softened

1 cup brown sugar

1 egg

1½ cups grated carrots

½ cup raisins

3 tablespoons lemon juice

1 cup flour

1 teaspoon baking powder

1 teaspoon baking soda

1 tablespoon hot water

Preheat oven to 350 degrees. Dissolve baking soda in hot water, then combine with all other ingredients. Stir thoroughly. Pour pudding into a 9x11-inch baking dish. Bake for 30 minutes. Serve warm.

ROASTED FRUIT IN CIDER

2 tablespoons walnut oil

¼ cup maple syrup

2 teaspoons balsamic vinegar

1 peach, pitted and sliced

1 apricot, pitted and sliced

1 pear, cored and sliced

1 apple, cored and sliced

⅓ cup chopped glazed mixed dried fruit

½ cup apple cider

2 tablespoons pecans, chopped

Heat oil in a large skillet over medium heat. Add maple syrup and balsamic vinegar. Add sliced fresh fruit. Cook, partially covered, until slightly tender, less than 10 minutes. Remove from heat. Stir in dried fruit and apple cider. Transfer roasted fruit to serving bowl. Sprinkle with chopped pecans.

MIDDLE EASTERN CINNAMON AND CLOVE TEA

6 cups fresh, cold water

5 cinnamon sticks

2 cloves

Teabags

Honey

Combine cinnamon sticks, cloves, and water in teapot or saucepan. Bring water to a boil, reduce heat, and simmer 13 to 15 minutes. Bring back to boil; pour into cups with a teabag. Garnish with cinnamon stick. Sweeten with honey, if desired.

INDEX

* Mrs. Hinn's recipes